Table of Contents

Chapter 5: Using Digital Leverage   (pg 30-37)

- Welcome to the Digital Age
- The Power of Digital Leverage
- Popular Digital Technologies Shaping Careers
- Why Digital Skills Matter
- Career Opportunities in Digital Marketing
- More Digital Career Paths
- Example: Teen Freelancing Success Story
- Flowchart: Your Path to a Digital Career
- Framework: How to Choose Your Digital Career
- Digital Skills, Roles & Action Plan

Chapter 6: Personal Education Plan   (pg 38-45)

- Table: PEP vs. Traditional Plans
- Why a PEP Matters for Teens
- Example: Jamal's PEP Pivot
- Core Elements of a PEP: Build Yours Step-by-Step
- Track Academic Performance and Progress
- Table: Sample Progress Tracker (Oct-Dec Quarter)
- Identify Unique Necessities
- Highlight Personal Advantages
- Table: Improvement Action Planner
- Crafting Your PEP: Step-by-Step Guide
- Real-World PEP in Action: Teen Spotlights
- Flowchart: Build Your PEP
- Tools & Resources for Your PEP

TABLE OF CONTENTS

Chapter 7: Real-Life Examples, Stories, and Case Studies of Teens (pg 47-53)

- The Rise of the Modern Teen Achiever
- Table: Historical vs. Modern Teen Achievers – Timeless Lessons
- Timeless Trailblazers: Teens Who Changed History
- Ten Modern Teen Trailblazers
- From Inspiration to Ignition
- Flowchart: Turn Story into Strategy

Chapter 8: GIG ECONOMY STRATEGIES FOR TEENS (pg 54-62)

- Theme: From Scroll to Side Hustle
- Introduction to the Gig Economy
- Real Teen Success Stories
- Identifying Beginner-Friendly Gigs
- Platform Guide
- Mini Table: Skill Match
- Pro Tip Table: Profile Dos & Don'ts
- Pricing, Negotiation & Client Communication
- Time & Task Management
- Flowchart: Gig Work Loop
- Growth & Sustainability
- 30-Day Challenge: Earn Your First $100

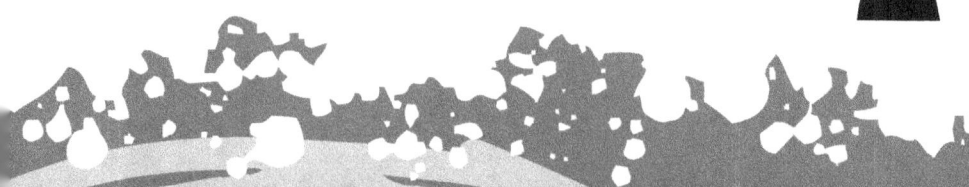

Learn Future Skills, Start Smart Gigs, Build Income Confidence, and Plan Your Dream Career Path

TEEN CAREER GUIDE 2026

BLUEPRINT FOR DIGITAL SKILLS, SIDE HUSTLES, AND REAL-WORLD SUCCESS

DR. FANATOMY

The TEEN CAREER GUIDE

BLUEPRINT FOR DIGITAL SKILLS, SIDE HUSTLES, AND REAL-WORLD SUCCESS

Learn Future Skills, Start Smart Gigs, Build Income Confidence, and Plan Your Dream Career Path

2026

Dr. Fanatomy

© Copyright 2025-26 - All rights reserved.

The content contained within this book may not be reproduced, duplicated, or transmitted without direct written permission from the author or the publisher.

Under no circumstances will any blame or legal responsibility be held against the publisher or author for any damages, reparation, or monetary loss due to the information contained within this book, either directly or indirectly.

Legal Notice:
This book is copyright-protected. It is only for personal use. You cannot amend, distribute, sell, use, quote, or paraphrase any part of the content within this book without the author's or publisher's consent.

Disclaimer Notice:
Please note that the information contained within this document is for educational and entertainment purposes only. Every effort has been made to present accurate, up-to-date, reliable, and complete information. No warranties of any kind are declared or implied. Readers acknowledge that the author is not engaged in the rendering of legal, financial, medical, or professional advice. The content within this book has been derived from various sources. Please consult a licensed professional before attempting any techniques outlined in this book.

By reading this document, the reader agrees that under no circumstances is the author responsible for any losses, direct or indirect, that are incurred as a result of the use of the information contained within this document, including, but not limited to, errors, omissions, or inaccuracies.

Bonus Booklet For You!

With great pleasure, I warmly welcome you to purchase the book. Congratulations on stepping towards improving yourself and developing the skills necessary to thrive as a teenager and beyond.

Below is a surprise gift for you!

Download it from the link (or scan the QR code below) - https://bit.ly/TeeNavigationBonus

Table of Contents

Introduction (pg 1-2)

- Introduction: Your Future Starts Here
- What Success Really Means Today
- Why This Blueprint Matters

Chapter 1: Self-Assessment and Understanding (pg 3-6)

- Why Self-Assessment Matters
- Two Ways to Assess Yourself
- How to Use Assessments the Smart Way
- Pro Tip: Reassess Often

Chapter 2: Start the Conversation (pg 7-12)

- Why Career Conversations Matter Now
- Then vs. Now — How Careers Have Changed
- The Problem with "Old Career Plans"
- Example: Alex's Wake-Up Call
- Mind Map: The Forces Shaping Future Careers
- A New Way to Work
- Example: Mia's Pivot
- Table: Risks & How to Handle Them
- Talking About Careers — Without the Pressure
- Micro-Conversation Tips
- Key Takeaway

Chapter 3: Career Fairs — Your Gateway to Opportunity

(pg 13-18)

- Why Career Fairs Matter in the Next 5 Years

Table of Contents

- Table: In-Person vs. Virtual Career Fairs
- How to Prepare for a Career Fair
- Flowchart: Career Fair Prep Roadmap
- Company Research Checklist
- Network Like a Pro
- Why You Should Attend Career Fairs
- How Career Fairs Work
- Update Your Resume Before the Fair
- Tips for Virtual Career Fairs

Chapter 4: Different Careers (pg 19-29)

- Choosing Your Path in a Changing World
- Career Categories Overview
- Why Career Exploration Matters Now
- Mind Map: From Interests to Career Categories
- Framework: The 5-Step Career Selection Blueprint
- Example Career Field: Animal Care
- Framework: The Career Fit Scorecard
- Flowchart: Your Career Decision Tree
- Top 10 Emerging Jobs for Teens
- Final Reflection: Design, Don't Drift
- Table: Sector Spotlight – Roles, Skills & Launchpads

TABLE OF CONTENTS

Chapter 9: GLOBAL MINDSET — THINK BEYOND BORDERS

(pg 63 -69)

- Quick Stat to Fuel Your World View
- What Is a Global Mindset?
- Understanding Cultural Differences
- Table: Feedback Styles by Country
- Working Across Time Zones and Languages
- Flowchart: Simple Flowchart
- Digital Citizenship and Etiquette
- Joining Global Opportunities
- Real Teen Success
- Reflection and Application
- Chapter Wrap-Up

Chapter 10: PASSION PROJECTS — TURN IDEAS INTO Impact

(pg 70 -77)

- Theme: Transform What You Love Into Real-World Change
- Quick Stat to Spark Your Fire
- Finding Your Cause or Idea
- Mind Map: From Passion to Impact
- Setting SMART Goals
- Mini Project Planner
- Flowchart: From Spark to Showcase
- Showcasing and Sharing
- Activity: 30-Day Impact Challenge
- Reflecting and Measuring Growth
- Turning It Into Portfolio Gold
- Chapter Wrap-Up

Table of Contents

Chapter 11: Appendix (pg 78 -87)

- Table A1: Fast-Growth Career Paths for Teens (No Degree Needed to Start)
- Table A2: Best Free Platforms to Learn In-Demand Digital Skills
- Table A3: Beginner-Friendly Gig Platforms for Teens (Age Requirements Included)
- Table A4: Quick Matching — Personality to Gig Type
- Table A5: Free Tools Every Teen Creator Should Know
- Table A6: Global Communication Cheat Sheet
- Table A7: 10 Passion Project Ideas Teens Can Start in One Week
- Table A8: College & Scholarship Essay Power Verbs (Use in Applications & Resumes)
- Table A9: Best Websites for Teen Internships & Remote Opportunities
- Table A10: Monthly Progress Reflection Prompt Set

Conclusion: Your Blueprint Is the Beginning (pg 88 - 89)

INTRODUCTION

Introduction: Your Future Starts Here

The world is changing faster than ever. New jobs are being created every day in areas like AI, climate tech, digital media, and the gig economy. By 2030, most careers will require strong digital skills, and millions of people will be working freelance or remotely.

That means the future isn't waiting for you—it's being built by you. You don't need to have your whole life figured out yet. But you do need to understand how to make smart choices, explore what excites you, and build the skills that will keep you ahead of the curve.

This book, The Teen Career Blueprint, is your guide to doing exactly that. It's not about picking one "perfect" job—it's about discovering who you are, learning how the world of work is evolving, and creating a path that's both flexible and fulfilling.

What Success Really Means Today

Success isn't just about landing a safe job or getting a steady paycheck anymore. It's about finding purpose, balance, and impact—doing work that matters to you and to the world.

Your generation values:
- Flexibility (remote work, digital freedom)
- Mental health and balance
- Sustainability and social good
- Creative independence

Whether you dream of being a content creator, app designer, climate researcher, or social entrepreneur, your career doesn't have to follow anyone else's script. You can mix skills, create opportunities, and even design jobs that don't exist yet. In the next few years, AI tools, freelancing platforms, and global connections will let you build your own path—on your own terms.

Why This Blueprint Matters

You're standing at a crossroads: school, plans, maybe college or a side hustle—and a thousand "what ifs." It's normal to feel unsure about what's next. The key is to start small: learn about yourself, test ideas, and adapt as the world changes.

This book gives you step-by-step tools to:

- ✅ Discover your strengths and interests
- ✅ Explore career paths that fit your personality
- ✅ Use digital tools and AI to your advantage
- ✅ Build real-world skills through gig work and projects
- ✅ Design a plan that grows with you

You don't have to figure it all out today. But starting now puts you ahead of most people.

Grab a notebook or open your notes app—your five-year head start begins now.

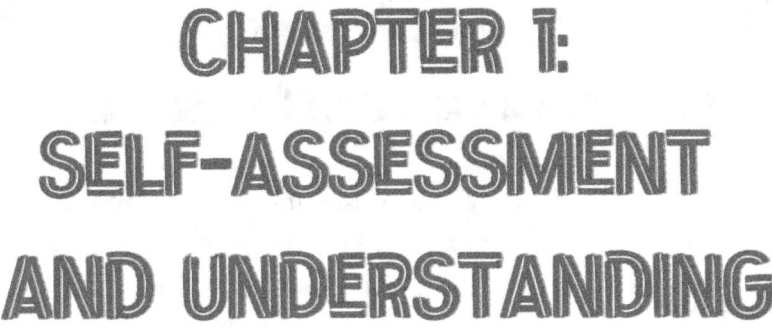

CHAPTER 1: SELF-ASSESSMENT AND UNDERSTANDING

Chapter 1: Self-Assessment and Understanding

If you want to create a future you love, the first step is simple: get to know yourself. Before choosing any major, internship, or side hustle, you need to understand what makes you you. Your interests, strengths, and values are your personal GPS—they guide you toward opportunities that actually fit.

Why Self-Assessment Matters

In the next few years, technology and careers will keep shifting. The jobs that exist today might look totally different by the time you graduate.

That's why understanding your personality and skills matters more than memorizing any career list.

Self-assessment helps you answer questions like:
- What kind of work makes me feel energized?
- What environments do I thrive in—structured or flexible?
- Do I prefer solving problems, creating things, or helping people?
- What values do I care about most—security, freedom, creativity, or impact?

When your choices match your values and interests, you'll feel more confident and motivated—because you'll be working with your strengths, not against them.

Two Ways to Assess Yourself

There are two main ways to explore your potential:
1. Formal Assessments – Quick online tests that analyze your skills, interests, or personality.
2. These can help you connect your results to career fields you may not have thought about before.
3. Self-Reflection – Slower but deeper. Journaling, talking with mentors, or even using an AI assistant (like ChatGPT) to analyze your hobbies and goals.

Example: If you love gaming, AI tools might help you discover careers in game design, cybersecurity, or virtual reality storytelling.

How to Use Assessments the Smart Way

These tools don't decide your future—they help you understand it.

Here's how to make them work for you:
- Take a mix of interest, skills, and values assessments.
- Write down your top results and look for patterns.
- Search for career paths that match your top skills and values.
- Ask: Which of these feel exciting, and which feel "meh"?

Your first step might not be your final destination—but every insight brings you closer to clarity.

Tool	What It Measures	Time	Best Use
O*Net Interest Profiler	Links your interests to 900+ careers	10 min	Find ideas for future careers or side gigs
16 Personalities Test	Shows how you think, work, and communicate	10–15 min	Understand your teamwork and creative style
VIA Character Strengths	Finds your top personal strengths	15 min	Connect values to meaningful careers
Traitify Assessment	Visual quiz about talents and creativity	5 min	Discover gig or freelance roles that fit you
FOCUS2	Matches interests, majors, and skills	30–45 min	Choose a college major or long-term plan
MBTI (Myers-Briggs)	Deep dive into personality preferences	20–30 min	Understand how you work best
Jung Typology Test	Fast version of MBTI	10 min	Quick overview of personality-career match

Try This Exercise
- Choose one of the tools above.
- Take the test and note your top results.
- Ask an AI tool:

"Suggest future careers that match my strengths in creativity and problem-solving."

- Write down the top 3 that sound exciting.
- Research each one for 10 minutes—see what skills they require.

That's your first mini–career map.

Pro Tip: Reassess Often
Your skills and interests will grow as you do. Take a new self-assessment every year—or after you learn something new. Think of it as updating your "career GPS."

Chapter 2: Start the Conversation

Why Career Conversations Matter Now

Let's be real — the future of work is changing faster than our TikTok feeds. AI, automation, and the gig economy are creating new jobs daily — while others disappear just as fast. In the next five years, millions of new AI-driven jobs will appear across industries, while millions of old ones fade away. So here's the truth: you can't plan your career like your parents did. The world isn't about climbing one ladder anymore — it's about building your own staircase, one skill at a time. Career talks aren't just for guidance counselors — they're for you. Talking about your goals, curiosities, and even confusions helps you figure out what kind of work actually fits you.

Then vs. Now – How Careers Have Changed

Aspect	Old Way (Pre-2020)	New Reality (By 2030)	What It Means for You
Job Path	One company for life	Multiple jobs, gigs, and side hustles	Build flexibility; try freelancing early
Entry Barriers	Diploma = job	Digital skills = entry ticket	Learn AI tools & online platforms
Opportunities	Local or regional	Global & remote	Connect with global teams online
Work Readiness	Post-grad focus	High school side hustles count	Start small — test your passions now
Growth Mindset	One direction	Constant reinvention	Keep learning; pivot often

The Problem with "Old Career Plans"

Old-school career planning doesn't work anymore. Most schools still teach skills for jobs that might not even exist soon. Automation, AI checkouts, and bots are replacing tasks once handled by humans — especially in entry-level roles. You can't just rely on a diploma; you need tech fluency, creativity, and adaptability. The good news? Those are your generation's superpowers.

Example: Alex's Wake-Up Call

Alex, 16, planned to work in retail after high school. But when AI checkouts took over, that plan collapsed. Instead of giving up, Alex turned his coding hobby into a strength — he built his first app prototype and landed a freelance project online.

Lesson: Career setbacks can be launchpads when you use your skills creatively.

Mind Map: The Forces Shaping Future Careers

Branches:

1. Globalization 🌍
   - Pros: Remote work with teams worldwide.
   - Cons: More competition — stay sharp and unique.
   - Action: Join online collabs or youth innovation groups.

2. Automation & AI 🤖
   - Machines are taking over routine jobs.
   - Action: Learn how to work with AI, not against it. Try prompt writing or digital design tools.

3. Collaboration
   - Most careers involve teamwork across platforms.
   - Action: Practice soft skills — communication, empathy, leadership — through group projects or volunteering.

4. Creativity & Adaptability
   - Creativity is your unfair advantage.
   - Action: Try content creation, digital storytelling, or a creative side hustle.

A New Way to Work

Forget the "safe job" myth. By 2030, multi-career lifestyles will be the norm — people will juggle creative gigs, remote work, and passion projects.

The rise of the creator economy means your hobbies can become careers. Love fashion? Sell designs online. Into gaming? Stream and learn content editing. Care about the planet? Build eco-focused digital products.

Example: Mia's Pivot

Mia wanted to be "an artist," but didn't know how. After experimenting with AI art tools, she designed sustainable digital fashion for online stores. What started as a weekend idea became a full-fledged side hustle by graduation.

Lesson: Small experiments can lead to big opportunities.

Table: Risks & How to Handle Them

Risk	Impact on Teens	Smart Strategy
Unemployment	Entry-level jobs shrinking	Build versatile skills; try micro-gigs on Fiverr or TaskRabbit
Insecurity	Freelance work = no guaranteed income	Create multiple income streams; save early
Inequality	Digital divide widens gaps	Learn free AI tools via Coursera or Khan Academy
Automation	Routine jobs replaced by tech	Focus on creativity, empathy, and analysis — skills AI can't copy
Mental Burnout	Overwork & hustle culture	Schedule "tech-free" hours weekly

Talking About Careers – Without the Pressure

Thinking about the future can feel heavy — especially with everyone asking, "So what do you want to be?" Instead of stressing about having one big answer, focus on small, open-ended conversations with yourself, your friends, or mentors.

Table : Conversation Starters That Actually Work

Prompt	Why It Works	What to Explore Next
"If you could build any app, what would it do?"	Sparks creativity	Design-thinking & coding skills
"What's the coolest AI trend you've seen lately?"	Builds awareness of innovation	Explore emerging tech careers
"What side hustle would you start if school didn't exist?"	Unlocks entrepreneurial ideas	Monetization paths
"What job would exist in your favorite movie universe?"	Adds fun & imagination	Creative storytelling industries
"What problem would you solve if you had $1M?"	Reveals values & priorities	Connect passions to purpose

Micro-Conversation Tips

- Keep it casual. A short walk or snack chat beats a long, formal talk.
- No judgment zone. Wild dreams lead to smart ideas.
- Ask yourself open-ended questions. Example: "What excites me most about the future of work?"
- Reflect weekly. Note one new insight in your digital planner.
- Stay curious. Watch interviews, listen to career podcasts, or join youth innovation clubs.

Key Takeaway

You don't need to have a five-year plan — just a five-minute conversation with yourself every week.

Ask, explore, test, repeat. That's how successful people build futures that evolve with them.

Your journey isn't about predicting the future — it's about creating it.

Action Step: This week, have one "future talk" — with a friend, teacher, or even an AI assistant. Record what inspires you. Your career blueprint is already forming.

CHAPTER 3: CAREER FAIRS — YOUR GATEWAY TO OPPORTUNITY

Chapter 3: Career Fairs – Your Gateway to Opportunity

Why Career Fairs Matter in the Next 5 Years

As hiring becomes increasingly hybrid every year, career fairs—now mostly virtual or blended—are becoming golden gateways for teens to meet real recruiters. By 2030, nearly 80% of employers are expected to use virtual fairs to connect with diverse, young talent. These events bridge the gap between you and prominent companies like Google, Tesla, and emerging startups in AI and green technology. Career fairs aren't just about getting a job—they're about showing up, standing out, and starting your journey.

Table : In-Person vs. Virtual Career Fairs

Aspect	In-Person Fairs	Virtual Fairs (Dominant by 2030)	Pro Tip for Teens
Attendance	Campus-based, local reach.	Global reach, 90% employer participation.	Pre-register on platforms like Brazen or Handshake.
Cost/Logistics	Travel-heavy; average cost $50–$200.	Zero travel; saves 80% of time and cost.	Use the savings for a professional headshot.
Networking	Booth visits and QR scans.	AI matchmaking and chat rooms.	Practice VR avatars for virtual fairs.

What Is a Career Fair?

A career fair (or job fair) is an event where employers, recruiters, and job seekers meet—either in person or online.

They're organized to save time for companies and help students like you gain direct access to potential employers. Expect smart tools like AI booth matching that connect you instantly with companies that fit your skills.

How to Prepare for a Career Fair

Preparation is your best armor. Start at least 2–3 weeks before the fair. Research, plan, and polish.

Flowchart: Career Fair Prep Roadmap

Career Fair Prep Flowchart

Start → Find Career Fair (Handshake / LinkedIn)

↓

Research (2 Weeks Out) → List 10+ Companies → Rank Top 5

↓

Customize Tools → Tailor Resume (3 Versions) → Craft 30-Second Pitch

↓

Logistics Check → Outfit / Tech Test → Pack Kit (Resumes, Notepad, Charger)

↓

Day-Of → Arrive Early / Log In → Network (5–7 Mins Each Booth)

↓

End → Follow Up Within 24 Hours (Thank-You Emails / LinkedIn)

Company Research Checklist

Fair Type	Do's (Essentials)	Don'ts (Avoid)	Why It Wins
In-Person	Smart casual: slacks, shirt, blazer.	Jeans, sneakers, flashy accessories.	Looks confident yet approachable.
Virtual	Solid top, clean background.	Pajamas or cluttered space.	Camera-ready and professional.
Eco-Focused	Sustainable fabrics, QR badge.	Synthetic overload.	Matches modern ESG values.

Network Like a Pro
- Prioritize your top 5 booths first.
- Keep eye contact and smile.
- Listen actively—don't just talk.
- Share your QR or contact card.
- Follow up within 24–48 hours.

Example

After a chat with a recruiter at a logistics company, a teen emailed:" Loved discussing green delivery AI—here's my resume and LinkedIn link. Can we continue the conversation over a virtual coffee?"

Result? An interview offer.

Why You Should Attend Career Fairs

Benefit	For Teens	For Employers	Future Edge (By 2030)
Direct Access	Meet dream companies.	Scan diverse young talent.	50% more interview invites.
Opportunities	Internships, gigs, full-time leads.	Faster hiring cycles.	Teen hiring up 40%.
Skill Practice	Improve networking confidence.	Gauge soft skills.	AI tools double match rate.
Information	Learn about culture, pay, and trends.	Gauge market interest.	Virtual saves 80% cost/time.

How Career Fairs Work

Think of a fair as a "career theme park" — full of booths, chats, and surprise opportunities.

Mind Map: Career Fair Flow

Central Node: Event Day
- Arrival/Check-In: QR code or online lobby.
- Booth Visits: Talk 5–10 min; pitch, ask, connect.
- Sessions/Workshops: Listen, take notes.
- Wrap-Up: Send thank-yous, connect on LinkedIn.

Update Your Resume Before the Fair

Tip	How-To	Example
Targeted Summary	Add 1-line goal matching fair type.	"Aspiring data analyst passionate about ethical AI."
Customized Versions	2–3 resumes (general + company-tailored).	Tech firm? Highlight coding projects.
Print + Digital	Bring 20 copies and a QR link.	"Scan to see GitHub or Canva portfolio."
Concise Format	Bullet points; measurable results.	"Automated reports, saving 10 hrs/week."

Tips for Virtual Career Fairs

Virtual events = real connections. Just bring your best digital self.

Flowchart: Virtual Fair Mastery Roadmap

Start → Register (Brazen / Zoom)
↓
Tech Audit → Check Mic, Camera, Internet
↓
Ready Content → Upload Resume & Practice Pitch
↓
Engage → Join Lobby → AI Match Booths → Chat 3–5 Mins Each
↓
Track → Spreadsheet of Contacts → Thank-You Message (24 Hrs)
↓
End → Connect on LinkedIn / Continue Networking

Final Thought

Career fairs—whether virtual or in-person—are not just job markets. They're where you find your voice, meet mentors, and start building your future.

By 2030, opportunities will flow more through digital fairs than job boards. Be ready, be bold, and take that first step with confidence.

🔍 Quick Recap: Your Career Fair Checklist
- Research 10+ companies
- Tailor 3 versions of your resume
- Practice your 30-second pitch
- Test your tech setup (for virtual fairs)
- Prepare follow-up messages

✅ Pro Tip: Every recruiter you meet is a doorway—your job is just to knock.

Chapter 4: Different Careers

Introduction: Choosing Your Path in a Changing World

The world of work is evolving faster than ever. Whether you're a teen starting to explore options or someone already experimenting with part-time jobs and projects, your career journey begins with one key step — self-awareness. Knowing what you enjoy, what you're good at, and what truly matters to you can help you find not just a job, but a purposeful path. The job market this year is nothing like it was five years ago. Artificial intelligence, automation, sustainability, and remote work are reshaping opportunities everywhere.

From designing virtual reality fashion to assisting in online healthcare, career possibilities are more flexible, tech-driven, and inclusive than ever before.

Quick Global Snapshot:
- 34% growth in AI and data-related roles
- 29% growth in cybersecurity and digital privacy jobs
- 18 million new green jobs projected worldwide
- Over 60% of teen-friendly jobs now offer flexible or hybrid options.

In this chapter, you'll:
1. Explore 20+ career categories using the current 2025 data.
2. Match your interests and skills (from Chapter 1's self-assessment).
3. Test your fit through short-term gigs, volunteering, or internships.

Your goal isn't to choose a job for life—it's to discover what fits your values and lifestyle right now.

Table: 2025-26 Career Categories Overview

(Based on U.S. BLS and ONET Data: Growth 2023–2033, Median Entry Salary for High School Grads or Early Learners)*

Category	Projected Growth	Median Entry Salary (2025)	Entry Requirements	2025 Trend Highlight
Animal Care	15%	$35,000	HS diploma; pet care certs	Tele-vet apps and mobile grooming
Art & Design	8%	$45,000	Portfolio; Adobe certs	AI-generated NFTs & AR fashion
Beauty & Well-Being	12%	$30,000	Cosmetology license	VR beauty tutorials & wellness influencers
Business & Finance	10%	$50,000	HS + finance courses	Fintech & crypto advising
Community & Voluntary	9%	$40,000	HS; coaching certs	NGO roles in climate advocacy
Computing & Tech	25%+	$60,000+	Coding bootcamps	AI/ML gigs via GitHub & Upwork

🧠 Tip: Visit ONET's "Bright Outlook" section for emerging roles like AI ethicists, digital wellness coaches, and sustainability analysts.*

Why Career Exploration Matters Now

Exploring careers early helps you make smarter decisions about school, skills, and goals. You don't need to have all the answers, but being curious gives you a powerful advantage. Think of this chapter as your career buffet — sample what interests you, reflect on what feels right, and come back for seconds when ready.

In the world ahead, "What do you want to be?" may no longer have one answer. Instead, teens are learning to ask:

"Which skills do I want to grow next?"

This flexible mindset is key to thriving in the next decade.

Mind Map : From Interests to Career Categories

Draw this on paper or in Canva! Start with "Your Passions" in the center.

Branch 1: Hands-On & Helpful
- Fields: Animal Care, Health, Emergency Services
- Why It Fits: You enjoy helping others and seeing results immediately.
- Trend: Remote care tech and wellness apps are expanding these jobs.

Branch 2: Creative & Storytelling
- Fields: Art, Design, Entertainment, Media
- Why It Fits: You love expressing ideas and creating something new.
- Trend: Digital art, AI design tools, and content creation careers are booming.

Branch 3: Tech & Numbers
- Fields: Computing, Engineering, Science, Finance
- Why It Fits: You enjoy problem-solving, logic, and precision.
- Trend: Entry-level AI and data roles now open to non-degree teens.

Branch 4: People & Business
- Fields: Marketing, Hospitality, Retail, Tourism
- Why It Fits: You thrive on interaction, leadership, and teamwork.
- Trend: Teens are launching online shops and microbrands on TikTok!

◎ Action: Circle your top 3 branches — these are your starting points.

Framework: The 5-Step Career Selection Blueprint

Step	Action	Tool/Example
1	Identify top 3 interests	Use Chapter 1's quiz results
2	Match to high-growth fields	See Table 4.1 & O*NET
3	Research entry paths	YouTube, Coursera, LinkedIn Learning
4	Try a mini gig or project	Fiverr, Rover, or volunteering
5	Review and reflect quarterly	Track in your "Career Journal"

🐾 Example Career Field: Animal Care

If you love pets, nature, or biology, this might be your calling. Animal care combines compassion with science and tech. From virtual vet apps to eco-pet services, it's becoming both meaningful and modern.

Job	Twist	Median Salary	Pros/Cons	Entry Path
Pet Sitter	App-based gigs via Rover	$35,000	Flexible; Irregular pay	HS + Pet CPR cert
Veterinary Tech	Drone pet monitoring	$40,000	Hands-on; Shift hours	2-year cert
Veterinarian	Tele-vet consultations	$100,000+	High impact; Long training	College + Vet school

Teen Story:
Alex, 17, used Midjourney to design sustainable t-shirts. His Etsy store went viral, earning $2,000/month and an art school scholarship.

💲 Example Career Field: Business & Finance
For those who love strategy, numbers, and leadership, business and finance roles are timeless yet constantly evolving.

Job	2025 Twist	Median Salary	Pros/Cons	Entry Path
Financial Adviser	Crypto & fintech guidance	$95,000	High income; Exam-heavy	Finance club; Khan Academy
Project Manager	AI-led agile teams	$90,000	Leadership; Stress	Junior PMP cert; volunteering

Teen Story:

Jordan started trading mock stocks in high school. His curiosity about markets led to a fintech internship by age 18.

🧠 Framework: The Career Fit Scorecard
Rate each field before diving in!

Factor	Question	Score (1-10)
Talent	What am I naturally good at?	☐
Interest	Does it excite me daily?	☐
Values	Does it match what I care about?	☐
Lifestyle	Does it fit my dream schedule?	☐
Growth	Is the field expanding (10%+)?	☐

⭐ 40+ points = Excellent Fit
💡 25–39 = Explore further
❗ Below 25 = Pivot to another field

Flowchart: Your Career Decision Tree

Start → Self-Assess (Chapter 1)
↓
Interest Identified? → Yes → List 3 Fields (Table 4.1)
↓
Skills Match? → Yes → Research Growth/Salary (BLS/O*NET)
↓
Values Align? → Yes → Try Mini Gig / Internship
↓
Demand Strong? (10%+ Growth) → Yes → Pursue Certifications or Training
↓
End → Reflect Quarterly → Update Goals

Table: Career Choice Factors

Factor	Key Question	Research Tip	Weight (1-10)
Talents	What am I naturally good at?	Review self-assessment	9
Interests	What motivates me daily?	Connect hobbies to jobs	10
Values	What purpose drives me?	Check company sustainability	8
Personality	Do I prefer people or projects?	MBTI/16Personalities test	7
Education	How much training do I need?	Coursera, Google, or Udemy	6
Salary	What's the minimum I'd be happy with?	BLS 2025 job calculator	7
Market Demand	Is this a high-growth field?	O*NET Bright Outlook	9

Top 10 Emerging Jobs for Teens

Job Title	Why It's Growing	Typical Start Path
AI Content Editor	AI needs human review for accuracy	Free AI ethics courses
Drone Operator	Used in delivery & emergency services	FAA drone certification
Sustainability Analyst	Green business focus	Online ESG courses
Esports Manager	Growth in competitive gaming	Volunteer at local tournaments
VR Experience Designer	Demand for immersive media	Unity/Blender basics
Cybersecurity Tester	Companies hire ethical hackers	CompTIA Security+
Digital Wellness Coach	Focus on mental health balance	Psychology & coaching certs
Data Entry Analyst	Entry into data science	Excel/Google Sheets mastery
Social Media Strategist	Brands seek Gen Z voices	Build personal brand
Remote Assistant	Admin roles online	Task management & communication skills

Final Reflection: Design, Don't Drift

The career world of 2025 is dynamic, decentralized, and full of possibilities. Instead of aiming for a single lifelong job, think of your path as a series of skill adventures. Each project, volunteer role, or side gig adds a layer to your experience and confidence.

"Your career isn't something you find — it's something you build, one step, one skill, and one experiment at a time."

So go ahead: explore, connect, and design your future with courage and curiosity.

Your first job doesn't have to be perfect — it just has to get you started.

Table: 2025-26 Sector Spotlight – Roles, Skills & Launchpads

(Based on BLS/ONET 2025 projections; entry-level pay ranges $40K–$60K for roles accessible to teens with certifications.)*

Sector: Computer Science & Technology

Job Profile	Key Skills (Top 3-4 for Teens)	Entry Path (Degree/Cert)	Fun Fact / Growth Edge
Coder / Software Developer	Python or Java, debugging, problem-solving, AI basics	HS + Coding Bootcamp (e.g., Codecademy 3-6 mo.)	25% growth; teens earn $1K/month via GitHub projects.
Data Center Expert	Cloud tools (AWS), troubleshooting, security basics	Associate's in IT or CompTIA Server+ ($300)	Remote data ops booming; $50K+ entry with certs.
Network Engineer	Networking (Cisco), firewalls, teamwork	HS + CCNA (6 mo. online)	10% growth; hybrid jobs maintaining AI infrastructure.
Cybersecurity Analyst	Ethical hacking, encryption, risk analysis	Bachelor's or CompTIA Security+ ($400)	32% growth; bug bounty teens earn $500 per find.

Sector: Healthcare

Job Profile	Key Skills (Top 3-4 for Teens)	Entry Path (Degree/Cert)	Fun Fact / Growth Edge
Nurse Assistant (CNA)	Patient care, empathy, basic medical software	HS + CNA Cert (4-6 weeks, ~$1K)	9% growth; telehealth CNA gigs rising.
Medical Coder	Medical terminology, billing software, accuracy	AAPC Cert (3 mo. online)	Remote coders earn $45K+; automation boosts accuracy.
Physical Therapy Aide	Exercise guidance, motivation, record-keeping	HS + PTA Aide Cert ($500)	15% growth; ideal for hands-on learners.
Health Informatics Specialist	Data analysis (EHR), privacy (HIPAA), tech use	Bachelor's or Online Cert (6 mo.)	17% growth; wellness app analytics growing.

💼 Sector: Business & Finance

Job Profile	Key Skills (Top 3-4 for Teens)	Entry Path (Degree/Cert)	Fun Fact / Growth Edge
Financial Analyst (Entry)	Excel, data viz, market research	Bachelor's or Google Data Analytics (6 mo.)	8% growth; fintech startups hiring student
HR Coordinator	Recruitment tools, diversity,	HS + SHRM Cert (3 mo. online)	Remote recruiting gigs now open for teens.
Entrepreneur / Small Biz Owner	Marketing, budgeting, customer service	No degree; Coursera startup courses	10% growth; Shopify teen stores earn
Sales Representative	Persuasion, CRM tools, negotiation	HS + HubSpot Sales Cert (free)	E-commerce sales roles exploding in 2025.

Sector: Creative Arts & Design

Job Profile	Key Skills (Top 3-4 for Teens)	Entry Path (Degree/Cert)	Fun Fact / Growth Edge
Graphic Designer	Adobe tools, typography, branding	HS + Adobe Cert (3 mo. online)	NFT and brand design gigs pay $500+.
Animator	3D modeling, storytelling,	Associate's or YouTube learning	8% growth; VR reels going viral.
Fashion Designer	Sketching, sustainability,	HS + Fashion Cert	Eco-fashion + resale booming.
Photographer	Lighting, editing, social media	HS + Online Photography Cert	Drone photo services trending.

Sector: Engineering & Manufacturing

Job Profile	Key Skills (Top 3-4 for Teens)	Entry Path (Degree/Cert)	Fun Fact / Growth Edge
Civil Engineering Tech	CAD, blueprint reading, surveying	Associate's in Civil Eng (2 yrs)	7% growth; $55K entry roles in green projects.
Electrical Engineer (Entry)	Circuit design, safety, problem-solving	Bachelor's or Apprenticeship	EV charging infrastructure
Mechanical Designer	3D printing, prototyping, teamwork	HS + SolidWorks Cert (2 mo.)	10% growth; robotics jobs for students.
Manufacturing Tech	Quality control, robotics basics	HS + Manufacturing Cert (6 mo.)	4% growth; smart factory jobs increasing.

Sector: Education & Training

Job Profile	Key Skills (Top 3-4 for Teens)	Entry Path (Degree/Cert)	Fun Fact / Growth Edge
Teacher Assistant	Classroom management, tech tools	HS + Paraeducator Cert	5% growth; after-school programs hiring.
Online Tutor	Subject mastery, digital communication	Subject Cert or TEFL	Remote boom; $20/hour average.
Corporate Trainer	Presentations, content design	Bachelor's or ATD Cert	6% growth; AI training modules needed.

Sector: Sustainability & Environmental Science

Job Profile	Key Skills (Top 3-4 for Teens)	Entry Path (Degree/Cert)	Fun Fact / Growth Edge
Environmental Technician	Fieldwork, sensors, GIS mapping	Associate's in Env Tech (2 yrs)	6% growth; $50K starting pay.
Renewable Energy Installer	Solar setup, safety, troubleshooting	HS + NABCEP Solar Cert (3 mo.)	Green jobs exploding (8%+).
Sustainability Analyst	Data analysis, policy research	Bachelor's in Env Science	10% growth; ESG roles trending.

Sector: Marketing & Communications

Job Profile	Key Skills (Top 3-4 for Teens)	Entry Path (Degree/Cert)	Fun Fact / Growth Edge
Social Media Manager	Analytics, creativity, trend spotting	HS + Meta Blueprint Cert	10% growth; influencer collabs pay $50K+.
Content Creator	SEO, storytelling, editing	No degree; YouTube/TikTok portfolio	Viral trends = ad revenue.
PR Specialist (Entry)	Writing, media monitoring, networking	Bachelor's or PR Cert	6% growth; social listening roles expanding.

Quick Start Guide: Your Next Move

- Rate each role 1–5 for "Excites Me?"
- Spot patterns — Do your interests combine?
- Example: Tech + Creative = UI/UX Designer
- Science + Helping = Health Data Specialist
- Journal your reflections — What energized you most?

"The best career isn't found—it's built, one project, one experiment, and one skill at a time."

CHAPTER 5: USING DIGITAL LEVERAGE

Chapter 5: Using Digital Leverage

Welcome to the Digital Age

Hey there, future changemaker!

The world we live in today is powered by screens, data, and connectivity. The digital revolution has completely transformed how we live, learn, work, and dream. With a tap or a swipe, you can connect with anyone, explore new opportunities, and even launch your own business—all before finishing high school.

The Internet has revolutionized life in once unimaginable ways. From instant access to global information to social media platforms shaping culture and careers, it has opened new doors in every field. But perhaps its greatest impact has been on career creation. Entire professions that didn't exist a decade ago—like digital influencers, app developers, or virtual event planners—are now booming.

Every teen today holds a powerful tool—the smartphone—that can also become their ticket to financial independence, creativity, and innovation. Let's explore how.

The Power of Digital Leverage

Using digital leverage means using technology, the Internet, and online platforms to create career opportunities, express creativity, and grow your personal brand. Whether you're learning a skill on YouTube, selling art on Etsy, writing a blog, or freelancing for clients overseas, you are already leveraging the digital world.

Popular Digital Technologies Shaping Careers

Technology	What It Does	Teen Career Edge
Artificial Intelligence (AI)	Machines that "think" and learn from data	Build AI art, chatbot design, or data tagging gigs
Machine Learning (ML)	Predicts outcomes using algorithms	Teens learn ML via Google's free AI courses
Blockchain	Secure digital transaction system	Ideal for crypto and digital finance explorers
Virtual & Augmented Reality (VR/AR)	Blends digital visuals with reality	Game design, 3D tours, immersive education
Internet of Things (IoT)	Smart devices that communicate	Smart home design or tech product testing
Digital Marketing	Promoting products online	Social media management, content creation
5G Networks	High-speed Internet	Boosts all online gig platforms and streaming work

Why Digital Skills Matter

Colleges, companies, and entrepreneurs now value digital literacy as highly as traditional academics. The more digitally skilled you are, the more opportunities you'll unlock—whether as a freelancer, business owner, or creative professional. Here are the core digital skills every modern teen should explore:

Digital Skill	Why It Matters	Tools to Learn
Social Media Management	Builds brand presence, boosts engagement	Hootsuite, Canva, Meta Creator Studio
SEO & SEM (Search Engine Optimization/Marketing)	Increases online visibility	Google Digital Garage, Semrush Academy
Content Creation & Writing	Powers blogs, videos, and brand storytelling	Medium, Grammarly, Notion
Data Analytics	Helps companies make smart decisions	Google Analytics, Excel, Power BI
Graphic Design & Video Editing	Shapes the look of the digital world	Adobe Photoshop, Canva, CapCut
Basic Coding	The foundation of tech innovation	Python (Codecademy), HTML/CSS
Email Marketing	Drives business conversions	Mailchimp, HubSpot Academy

Career Opportunities in Digital Marketing

Digital marketing is one of the fastest-growing fields, with millions of opportunities for students who love creativity and communication. Let's break down a few options:

1. Content Writing & Marketing

If you enjoy writing, storytelling, or researching new ideas, content writing is a fantastic starting point.

You can write blogs, social media posts, newsletters, or even ghostwrite eBooks. As your experience grows, you can move into content marketing—planning and managing campaigns that attract readers and customers.

Example:

A 17-year-old blogger from New Jersey wrote about teen finance tips on Medium—and now earns through affiliate links and sponsored posts.

2. Social Media Executive

If you live on Instagram or TikTok, why not get paid for it?
Businesses hire social media executives to plan, post, and interact with followers across platforms. You'll need creativity, consistency, and a sense of what trends are rising.
- Skills: Graphic design, analytics, and storytelling
- Tools: Canva, Later, Buffer

3. SEO Specialist

An SEO expert behind the scenes influences every Google search you make.

SEO (Search Engine Optimization) helps websites rank higher, attract more visitors, and convert them into customers.

If you enjoy analyzing keywords and identifying patterns, SEO is a perfect fit for you.

- Pathway: Learn basics via Google's free SEO course → Practice optimizing a blog → Apply for junior SEO gigs on Fiverr.

4. Graphic Designer or Videographer

Got an eye for design or enjoy making short videos?

Digital creatives are in huge demand—whether for YouTube channels, Instagram Reels, or brand marketing. Teens can start by creating digital posters, animations, or editing short films for student groups.

- Pro Tip: Join contests on platforms like 99designs or Behance to showcase your portfolio.

5. Digital Advertising

From YouTube ads to Instagram promotions, digital ads drive modern marketing.

You can learn how to plan ad campaigns, manage budgets, and target audiences.

Ad specialists earn well and work remotely for clients across the globe.

More Digital Career Paths

Career	What You'll Do	Why It Rocks
Affiliate Marketer	Promote products online & earn commission per sale	Passive income from blogs & social media
Kindle Author (KDP)	Self-publish your own books on Amazon	Creative freedom + royalty income
Digital Influencer	Build an audience and collaborate with brands	Fame + business partnerships
Freelancer	Offer digital services like writing, coding, or design	Work anywhere, anytime, with global clients

Example: Teen Freelancing Success Story

A high-school student passionate about gaming began writing reviews for a gaming blog. Within six months, he started getting paid gigs through Fiverr and eventually built a steady $500/month income—all from home.

Flowchart: Your Path to a Digital Career

Start → Identify Your Skill (Writing / Design / Coding / Marketing)
↓
Learn Online → Free Courses (Google, Coursera, YouTube)
↓
Create Samples → Build Portfolio (Blog / Instagram / GitHub)
↓
Freelance → Join Fiverr / Upwork / Internships
↓
Grow & Monetize → Brand Deals / Clients / Passive Income
↓
End → Turn Passion into Profession

Mind Map: Digital Leverage Opportunities

Digital Leverage
→ Digital Marketing
→ SEO / SEM / Content Creation
→ Creative Careers
→ Design / Video / Writing
→ Tech-Driven Roles
→ AI / Data Analytics / Coding
→ Entrepreneurial Paths
→ Affiliate Marketing / Kindle / Freelancing / Influencing

Framework: How to Choose Your Digital Career

Step	Question to Ask Yourself	Example
1. Identify Passion	What do I love doing online?	"I enjoy editing videos."
2. Match with Skill	What am I already good at?	"I'm creative and tech-savvy."
3. Explore Market Demand	What careers are growing?	"Social media and content marketing."
4. Start Small	Can I do this part-time?	"Yes, I can start a small page."
5. Monetize Wisely	How can I earn from it?	"Sponsored posts and freelance gigs."

Try This!
- Create a digital portfolio showcasing your top three skills.
- Apply for one freelance gig or internship this month.
- Write a short journal entry on how digital skills could shape your dream career.

Digital Skills, Roles & Action Plan

Category	Key Data/Insight (2025)	Teen Takeaway	Next Step for You
Global Gig Economy	$1.5 trillion in earnings; 73M US freelancers	Gen Z leads freelancing (52% active)	Create your Upwork profile and add 3 skill tags today.
AI Job Expansion	97 million new digital jobs forecast	AI literacy = career currency	Take a free AI course (Google/DeepLearning.ai) this week.
Top Skill Demand	SEO, AI, and social media up 25–50% in 2 years	Teens mastering 1 digital skill earn $20–40/hr	Pick 1 skill from Table 5.2 and practice 1 hr/day.
Entry-Level Income Potential	$500–$2,000/month for active teens	Freelance = early financial freedom	Choose 1 gig path (Table 5.4) and execute first task in 7 days.
Digital Creator Boom	90M+ KDP users; 1B+ content creators	You can monetize creativity, not just code	Publish 1 blog, short eBook, or post/week to grow visibility.
Sustainability of Skills	85% of 2030 jobs need digital fluency	Every effort now builds future readiness	Track progress in "My Gig Journal" and reflect weekly.

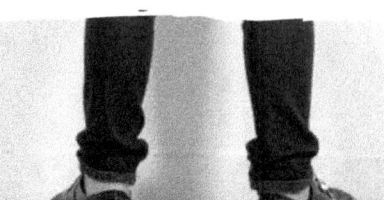

CHAPTER 6 :
PERSONAL EDUCATION PLAN

Chapter 6: Personal Education Plan

In this era, where AI tutors personalize lessons in real-time and 70% of high schoolers use apps like Duolingo or Khan Academy for self-paced learning, a Personal Education Plan (PEP) isn't just paperwork—it's your teen's customizable GPS for career success. Think of it as a dynamic roadmap, blending academic goals with gig-ready skills like prompt engineering or sustainable design, amid trends like microcredentials (short certs boosting resumes by 25% for Gen Z) and hybrid schooling. For teens in transition—high school to college/gigs—PEPs bridge gaps, with 2025 data showing students with tailored plans 40% more likely to pursue aligned careers. Co-owned by students, parents, schools, and mentors (government-backed in programs like Florida's PEP ESA), it tracks progress, spotlights strengths, and flags improvements—ensuring no one's left navigating blind. In a world where 85% of jobs demand digital fluency, your PEP turns "what's next?" into "I've got this." Let's blueprint yours—start with a journal, end with a gig.

Table: PEP vs. Traditional Plans

Aspect	Traditional Plan (One-Size-Fits-All)	PEP (Personalized)	Teen Benefit Example
Structure	Rigid curriculum; annual reviews.	Flexible, AI-updated quarterly.	Swap algebra for coding if AI's your jam—frees time for freelance.
Focus	Grades only.	Academics + skills/career goals.	Track robotics club toward engineering cert, not just GPA.
Tools	Textbooks/paper.	Apps (e.g., Notion AI, Coursera).	VR simulations for med careers; 30% faster skill gain.
Involvement	Teacher-led.	Student/parent/mentor collab.	You lead: "I want esports management"—family votes on electives.
Outcomes	Diploma path.	Career readiness (e.g., 21% higher job fit).	Microcreds like Google IT Support land $50K gigs pre-college.

Why a PEP Matters for Teens

Teens face unprecedented flux: 97 million new AI/green jobs by 2025, but 85 million displaced—PEPs equip you to pivot. During transitions (e.g., 9th to 10th grade or post-HS), they decode learning needs amid hybrid models (60% schools blended) and sustainability mandates (ESG in 70% curricula). Shared duty (schools/govt via ESAs like Florida's PEP, funding $8K+ for homeschoolers) ensures equity—e.g., low-income teens access VR tools for global skills. Result? 50% better retention in career-aligned paths, per 2025 edtech reports. Tie it to your book blueprint: Ch. 1 assessments feed goals; Ch. 4 careers shape electives.

Example: Jamal's PEP Pivot

Jamal, a 16-year-old in Florida's PEP program, struggled with standard math but aced robotics club. His ESA-funded plan swapped algebra for AI coding (via Coursera microcred), adding mentorship from Polygence. By spring, he prototyped a sustainability app, landing a $500 freelance gig—proving PEPs turn "flunks" to futures

Core Elements of a PEP: Build Yours Step-by-Step

A PEP is your living doc—update quarterly via apps like Notion or Google Docs. Below, expand each element with 2025 relevance, plus a sample template.

Track Academic Performance and Progress

Log wins/gaps— apps like Gradescope AI auto-grade, freeing time for gigs. Element Tip: Beyond GPA, track soft skills (e.g., "Led debate = leadership").

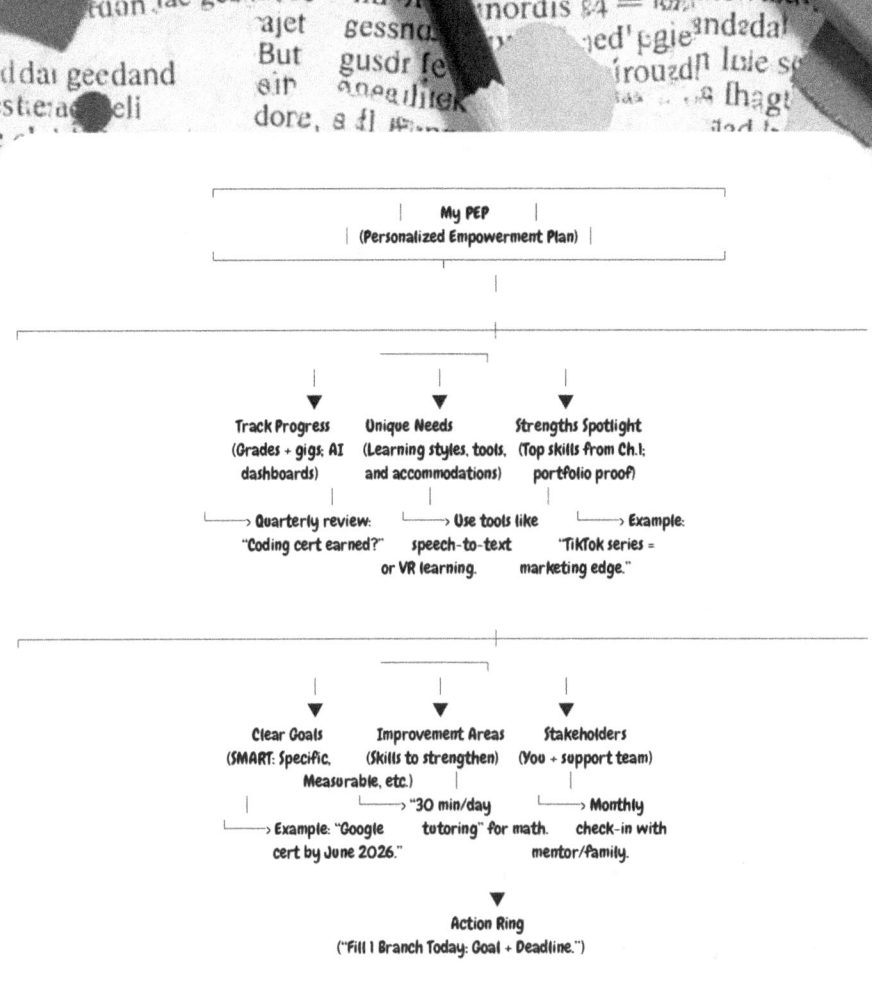

Table : Sample Progress Tracker (Oct-Dec Quarter)

Area	Baseline (Oct)	Goal (Dec)	Milestones (Nov)	Progress %	Notes/Resources
Academics (GPA)	3.2	3.5	Complete 2 electives	60%	AI tutor app (Duolingo for
Skills (Coding)	Beginner	Python Cert	5 projects on GitHub	40%	Free Codecademy; mentor meet #1.
Career (Gig)	None	1 Freelance Job	Profile on Upwork	70%	Fiverr bids; $100 target.
Well-Being	Stressed	Weekly Breaks	Yoga 3x/week	80%	Calm app; family walk logs.

Example:

Sofia tracked her PEP via Notion in fall 2025—spotted writing strength, shifting to journalism elective, scoring her first paid article ($50).

Identify Unique Necessities

Spot custom needs—2025's neurodiversity focus (e.g., 1 in 5 teens with ADHD) means tools like AI captions for dyslexics. Tip: Involve counselors for ESAs funding VR for kinesthetic learners.

Highlight Personal Advantages

Amplify Ch. 1 strengths—e.g., "Empathy = counseling fit." 2025: Portfolios via LinkedIn showcase teen advantages like digital nativity.

Example:
In a 2025 Polygence program, Liam highlighted his VR hobby in PEP, securing mentorship for game design—leading to a microcred and internship.

Define Objectives Clearly

SMART goals rule: Specific (e.g., "Earn Google Analytics cert"), Measurable (track via app), Achievable (free resources), Relevant (ties to Ch. 4 career), Time-bound (by Q2 2026). 2025 Trend: Career readiness schools like Cascade Virtual integrate CRE (Career Readiness Education) for 20% better outcomes.

Identify Areas Needing Improvement

Gap-spot: Weak public speaking? Toastmasters app. 2025: AI coaches like Yoodli provide instant feedback, cutting practice time by 50%.

Table: Improvement Action Planner

Weak Area	Why Improve? (Career Link)	Action Steps (2025 Tools)	Timeline	Success Metric
Math for Data Roles	Analytics jobs need it.	Khan Academy AI modules; 20 min/day.	Nov	80% on practice quizzes.
Networking	Gig opps via LinkedIn.	Handshake app; 1 connect/week.	Deec	10 new contacts; 1 coffee chat.

Identify Involved Parties and Accountability

Team up: You (lead), parents (support), school counselor (review), mentor (e.g., via Big Brothers Big Sisters). 2025: Apps like Trello for shared dashboards ensure accountability—quarterly sign-offs.

Example 6.4: A Florida PEP family in 2025 used shared Google Docs for reviews—teen's mentor flagged coding gaps, unlocking ESA funds for bootcamp, boosting confidence 30% (self-reported).

Crafting Your PEP: Step-by-Step Guide

PEPs evolve—review biannually, adapt to trends like VR learning (adopted by 40% schools).

Real-World PEP in Action: Teen Spotlights

- Example: Aria's Hybrid Hustle Aria, 17, in a CRE school like Cascade Virtual, used her PEP to blend HS with esports management certs (funded via ESA). Quarterly reviews via Zoom tracked progress—swapped history for VR design, landing a $300 tournament gig by fall 2025.
- Example: Self-Guided Success Per Polygence 2025 guides, self-motivated teen Kai built a PEP around biotech research, using free edtech like Labster VR—secured mentorship, publishing a paper snippet on arXiv.

Flowchart: Build Your PEP

```
Start: Self-Assess (Ch. 1 Tools)
              │
              ▼
Gather Team (You + Parents/Counselor)
              │
              ▼
      Brainstorm Goals
              │
              ├──→ SMART Check?
              │        │       │
              │        ├── Yes → Log in Doc/App
              │        └── No → Refine
              │
              ▼
   Map Elements (Table 6.2 Tracker)
              │
              ▼
    Identify Strengths & Needs
              │
              ▼
   Add Resources (Free Certs / ESAs)
              │
              ▼
   Set Accountability (Monthly Meets)
              │
              ▼
       Review Quarterly
              │
              ▼
  Adapt Plan (e.g., Add AI Course)
              │
              ▼
End: Signed & Shared – Gig Goal Set!
```

Tools & Resources for Your PEP

- Apps: Notion AI (free templates), Gradescope (auto-feedback).
- Programs: Florida PEP ESA ($8K for homeschool; apply via Step Up).
- Free Certs: Google Career Certificates (6 months, job guarantee).
- Mentorship: Polygence (teen-led projects, $2K avg but scholarships)

Call to Action:

Draft your PEP today—use the template, flowchart your first goal, and schedule a family review. By 2026, it'll be your career superpower. What's your #1 objective? Write it now!

Table: Key Components of a Personal Education Plan (PEP)

Component	Description	Actionable Steps for Teens	Useful Tools / Examples
Academic Goals	Short- and long-term learning targets aligned with interests and future careers.	Set 3–5 goals per semester; review monthly; adjust based on progress.	Khan Academy progress dashboard; Duolingo for language streaks.
Strengths & Skills Inventory	Identifies natural strengths and developing skills useful for school, careers, and side gigs.	Take a strengths quiz; highlight 3 skills to improve; practice weekly.	VIA Strengths Survey; Coursera skill badges; Adobe Express tutorials.
Learning Needs & Supports	Personalized support strategies to overcome gaps, challenges, or learning barriers.	Note challenges (e.g., time, focus, resources) and request help early.	Khanmigo AI tutor; teacher/mentor check-ins; Pomodoro timer apps.
Career & Postsecondary Pathways	Clear roadmap to college, trades, entrepreneurship, or gig-based work.	Explore 2–3 possible paths; try mini-gigs or short courses related to each.	LinkedIn Learning certificates; school career counselor folders.
Progress Tracking & Reflection	Consistent review to measure growth and maintain motivation.	Do a monthly or quarterly reflection; celebrate small wins.	Shared Notion page; Google Docs reflection journal; Calendar reminders.

Table : Data-Driven Benefits of a PEP for Career Success

Benefit	Key Statistic	Impact on Teens	Source Insight
Higher Engagement in Self-Paced Learning	63% of K–12 students use online learning tools daily (up from 50% in 2021).	Supports hybrid schooling and builds independence in skill-building.	Devlin Peck Online Learning Stats; EdTech Adoption Reports.
Stronger Resumes Through Microcredentials	96% of employers value microcredentials; 85% of earners report improved career opportunities.	Quick skill certificates make teens stand out in early job and gig markets.	Forbes Future of Work Survey; Lumina Foundation Report.
Improved Career Confidence & Alignment	Students with personalized learning plans are 40% more likely to pursue aligned careers.	Reduces anxiety about "what's next" and boosts purpose and clarity.	ECMC Foundation Gen Z Career Readiness Survey.
Essential Digital Skill Readiness	92% of jobs now require basic to advanced digital skills.	Teens gain practical job readiness and gig-market advantage.	National Skills Coalition; RAND Technology Workforce Brief.

CHAPTER 7 :
REAL-LIFE EXAMPLES, STORIES, AND CASE STUDIES OF TEENS

Chapter 7: Real-Life Examples, Stories, and Case Studies of Teens

The Rise of the Modern Teen Achiever

A century ago, "teenager" wasn't even a word. You were either a child or an adult-in-training. But in 2025, the teen years have become a launchpad.

Artificial intelligence, digital media, and the gig economy have blurred the line between learning and earning. More than 52 percent of Gen Z now freelances—designing apps, editing videos, selling products, or tutoring online. Over 73 million people under 25 are earning independently through TikTok Shops, Etsy stores, and Upwork gigs.

This chapter celebrates that momentum. You'll meet the bold teens of history —Alexander, Joan, and Mary—who proved youth has always held power. Then you'll meet ten modern changemakers who are proving it again through science, entrepreneurship, activism, and creativity.

Each story connects directly to the career-planning tools you've been building in previous chapters—self-assessment (Ch. 1), confidence (Ch. 2), networking (Ch. 3), career exploration (Ch. 4), digital leverage (Ch. 5), and personal-evolution planning (Ch. 6).

Table : Historical vs. Modern Teen Achievers – Timeless Lessons

Trait	Historical Example	Modern Parallel (2025)	Career Tie-In
Bold Vision	Alexander the Great – Conquered at 20	Teen tech founders solving AI ethics	Ch. 2 Dream Big; Pivot Smart

Trait	Historical Example	Modern Parallel (2025)	Career Tie-In
Defiant Courage	Joan of Arc – Led armies at 17	Activists fighting climate denial	Ch. 4 Values-Driven Careers
Creative Genius	Mary Shelley – Wrote Frankenstein at 19	Teen coders building VR worlds	Ch. 5 Digital Innovation
Resilience	Each faced extreme odds	Entrepreneurs bootstrapping from $0	Ch. 6 Quarterly PEP Pivots

Timeless Trailblazers: Teens Who Changed History

Alexander the Great (356-323 BC) – Vision in Action

By twelve, Alexander tamed the wild horse Bucephalus, a moment that revealed natural leadership. Tutored by Aristotle, he studied philosophy and science while commanding troops in his father's absence. When he became king at 20, he built one of the largest empires ever known.

Lesson: Strategy + Learning = Power. Just as Alexander mastered maps and mentors, you can map your digital empire through guided self-assessment (Ch. 1) and active networking (Ch. 3).

Joan of Arc (1412-1431) – Courage Under Fire

At 17, Joan convinced generals to follow her into battle and helped France win the Siege of Orléans. Her defiance of gender rules cost her life but sparked movements that still inspire courage.

Lesson: Speak up for what matters. Today's climate strikers and social advocates echo Joan's spirit. Use Ch. 2's confidence tools to find your own mission and rally others online.

Mary Shelley (1797-1851) - Creativity Unleashed

At 19, Mary Shelley wrote Frankenstein—a story about human creation and responsibility that predicted modern AI debates. She transformed loneliness and loss into imagination.

Lesson: Creativity turns pain into progress. Follow her lead through Ch. 6's PEP routine: write, design, or build something small every day.

Ten Modern Teen Trailblazers

Ten real teens, ten different paths—proof that passion and planning can start now.

(1) Emily Chen, 17 - AI Pioneer in Healthcare

- Achievement: Developed an AI tool that detects pancreatic cancer early with 92 % accuracy, earning a 2025 Regeneron STS finalist spot.
- Journey: Emily began during lockdown with free Coursera AI courses and a community hackathon. Rejected grants didn't stop her; she open-sourced her code and drew 5 K GitHub stars.
- Career Lesson: Persistence beats perfection. Tech + empathy can save lives.
- Gig Hack: Freelance AI prompt design on Fiverr ($20/hr).
- Result: $100 K scholarship and pilot tests in clinics.

2. Toby Brown, 16 - Fintech Kid Boss

- Achievement: Founded Beem, a teen-banking app using AI budgeting; raised $2 M seed funding and hit 100 K users.
- Journey: Frustrated by money stress at home, Toby taught himself code through Codecademy and tested prototypes at school fairs.
- Career Lesson: Solve everyday problems—you'll never run out of customers.
- Gig Hack: Test new apps for pay ($50–100).
- Result: Forbes 30 Under 30 honoree by 17.

3. Aisha Patel, 15 – Eco Alchemist

- Achievement: Created biodegradable plastic from algae, breaking down 80 % faster than petroleum-based plastic; 3M Young Scientist Challenge finalist.
- Journey: Inspired by beach cleanups, she ran DIY experiments in her garage and used Ch. 6's PEP plan to blend science with sustainability.
- Career Lesson: Combine curiosity + cause = career.
- Gig Hack: Sell eco-STEM kits on Etsy ($10–20).
- Result: Patent pending and $25 K grant.

4. Jordan Lee, 18 – VR Visionary

- Achievement: Built a VR education platform for underserved schools; won JA Titan Challenge ($50 K).
- Journey: Self-taught VR editing from YouTube, then networked at ed-tech fairs to find partners.
- Career Lesson: Merge teaching and tech for impact.
- Gig Hack: Tutor VR skills on Outschool ($15/hr).
- Result: 10 K students reached; full-time founder.

5. Sofia Ramirez, 16 – Climate Crusader

- Achievement: Built a carbon-tracking app adopted by 50 schools; named UN Youth Delegate 2025.
- Journey: Merged love for coding with climate advocacy through online bootcamps and school campaigns.
- Career Lesson: Technology can amplify activism.
- Gig Hack: Offer eco-audits for local businesses ($30).
- Result: Policy influence and global recognition.

6. Kai Nguyen, 17 – Mental Health Maverick
- Achievement: Created an AI chatbot for teen anxiety; reached 1 M downloads and secured $200 K funding.
- Journey: Built a prototype after losing a friend to stress; refined ethics and empathy using PEP reviews.

- Career Lesson: When tech meets heart, change follows.
- Gig Hack: Beta-test mental-health apps ($100/project).
- Result: Forbes 30 Under 30 2024; MIT research offer.

7. Lila Voss, 14 – Fashion Rebel

- Achievement: Turned thrifted clothes into sustainable streetwear, earning $10 K in sales and the Inno Under 25 award.
- Journey: Mixed art-class sketches with business sense from YouTube tutorials.
- Career Lesson: Creativity + Commerce = Freedom.
- Gig Hack: Sell custom tees or re-designs on Depop/Etsy ($20).
- Result: Collaboration with H&M eco-line.

8. Marcus Hale, 15 – Bee Guardian

- Achievement: Designed urban beehives, increasing city pollination by 30 %; earned President's Environmental Youth Award.
- Journey: Started with the school gardening club, then partnered with local apiaries.
- Career Lesson: Hands-on STEM counts too.
- Gig Hack: Teach beekeeping workshops ($50 per session).
- Result: Expanding model to urban farms nationwide.

9. Nora Kim, 17 – Podcast Powerhouse

- Achievement: Produced Future Bound, an ed-tech podcast for immigrant kids; 50 K downloads and sponsorship deals.
- Journey: Turned love for storytelling into audio skills via Anchor and CapCut.
- Career Lesson: Communication creates connection.
- Gig Hack: Guest on teen pods or voice-over projects ($100).
- Result: Youth media ambassador and startup mentor.

10. Riley Santos, 16 – Drone Dynamo

- Achievement: Built drones for disaster relief; won $75 K grant from Swarajya Young Innovators.
- Journey: Began with the school robotics club and YouTube engineering channels.
- Career Lesson: Innovation serves people best when it solves real problems.
- Gig Hack: Sell drone aerial footage for events ($200).
- Result: NGO partnerships across Asia.

From Inspiration to Ignition

Across centuries, every teen success story shares a pattern:
1. Vision – See a problem worth solving.
2. Courage – Take the first risk.
3. Creativity – Find your unique angle.
4. Resilience – Keep pivoting when it gets hard.

Flowchart: Turn Story into Strategy

Start → Pick one teen story that inspires you
↓
Reflect → Which trait matches your strengths (Ch. 1)?
↓
Adapt → Add a modern twist for your community
↓
Act → Set a PEP goal + first digital step (Ch. 6)
↓
Track → Review progress in 30 days
↓
Share → Post your mini-success and inspire others

Your Next Move

History and headlines both say the same thing: Age doesn't limit impact—mindset does. Every empire, invention, and startup began with a curious question.

CHAPTER 8 :
GIG ECONOMY STRATEGIES FOR TEENS

54

Chapter 8: GIG ECONOMY STRATEGIES FOR TEENS

⭐ Theme: From Scroll to Side Hustle

Picture this: your TikTok edits or math hacks turning into real cash — on your schedule.
 This chapter bridges the digital skills you developed in Chapter 5 and your self-knowledge from Chapter 1 into real-world earning power.
 Inspired by the teen boss moves from Chapter 7, this is your starter kit for flexible gigs that build into that killer portfolio in Chapter 9.
No fluff — we move from:
- Why hype? (intro spark)
- How start? (pick & setup)
- How crush? (ops & balance)
- How to level up? (scale & glow).

Everything's short, snappy, and updated teen trends.
 Let's turn "bored scroll" into "bank glow-up."

⚡ Quick Stat to Spark Your Hustle

💲 The global gig economy is projected to hit $582 billion in 2025 — and Gen Z teens are driving the boom with flexible digital side wins.

Introduction to the Gig Economy

Whoa, slow your scroll — gigs aren't "extra chores." They're your ticket to freedom in a world that rewards skill, speed, and creativity.

What Is the Gig Economy?
 Short-term, app-powered work like designing logos, tutoring online, or virtual pet-sitting — no boss, all you.

55

Why It Works for Teens:
- Fits around homework — no 9-to-5 drag.
- Builds real-world skills fast.
- Creates independence (hello, sneaker fund).
- Turns your hobbies into paydays.

Real Teen Success Stories:
- Alex, 13, earned her first $1K on Fiverr designing logos from doodles.
- Josh, 16 — made $1,000/month creating Instagram content for small brands.
- Shazil, 15 — turned his first $15 gig into a full graphic design business.
- Shaurya, 16 — used gig deadlines to fund his laptop and learn time mastery.

❈ Fact:
36% of Gen Z teens (ages 13–24) are already earning from digital gigs.

Bridge to Next:
Ready to match your Chapter 1 personality to your dream gig? Let's find your fit.

Identifying Beginner-Friendly Gigs

Feeling overwhelmed? Don't. Start with you-shaped gigs — no resume, just raw skill.

◎ Overview of Gig Types

Type	Description	Example
Creative	Design, editing, voiceovers	Fiverr, Canva services
Technical	Coding, testing apps	Upwork, Greenlight
Tutoring	Teaching peers online	Wyzant, Outschool
Social Media	Trend tracking, posting	Instagram, TikTok collabs
Micro-Tasks	Surveys, reviews	Swagbucks, Greenlight

🧠 Platform Guide

- Fiverr (13+) – Best for creative gigs (with parental consent).
- Upwork (18+) – Great for pros; observe project listings early.
- TaskRabbit (18+) – Local gigs (or try Nextdoor alternatives).
- Greenlight (13+) – Teen-safe app for surveys and micro-jobs.
- 🔒 Safety First: Always involve parents when setting up for 18.

❇️ Mini Quiz – What's Your Gig Zone?

Answer "Yes" or "No" to these five:
1. Love doodling or editing videos?
2. Math or coding comes easily?
3. Enjoy explaining stuff to friends?
4. Obsessed with TikTok trends?
5. Like quick app or review tasks?

Mostly 1s → Creative gigs
Mostly 2s → Technical gigs
Mostly 3s → Tutoring
Mostly 4s → Social media
Mostly 5s → Micro-tasks

Mini Table: Skill Match

Your Skill (from Ch. 5)	Possible Gig	Platform
Graphic Design	Logo creation	Fiverr
Social Media Savvy	Trend reports	Upwork
Math Whiz	Virtual tutoring	Wyzant
Writing Skills	Blog ghosting	Freelancer
Fast Learner	App testing	Greenlight

Building Your First Gig Profile

Time to flex your brand!

Writing an Eye-Catching Bio
- Keep it short and bold — 2–3 lines max.
- Example:

"15yo video edit ninja turning clips into viral gold — fast, fresh, and fearless."

Profile Images & Work Samples
- Use a clear, natural headshot (no heavy filters).
- Mock sample work in Canva or Google Slides.
- Upload 3–5 examples.

Use Testimonials
Get mini quotes from teachers, parents, or peers:
"Jordan's editing tips turned my project into an A+!"

🔍 Pro Tip Table: Profile Dos & Don'ts

✅ Do	🚫 Don't
Use action verbs ("Completed 10+ edits")	Write long bios (keep <150 words)
Add fun detail ("Gamer girl gone graphic")	Upload blurry selfies
Include keywords ("SEO writing," "YouTube editing")	Forget to list your top skills

Pricing, Negotiation & Client Communication

You're not "asking for work." You're offering value.

💰 Setting Your Rates
- Start at $10–15/hour or $20–40 per project.
- Never underprice your time — confidence sells.

🔄 Handling Feedback
- Welcome feedback like a pro:
- "Thanks for the note! I'll adjust and re-upload."
- Rule: 2 free revisions → $5 for extras.

🚫 Avoid Scams
- No off-platform payments.
- Check for verified badges.
- Report "pay-after" red flags immediately.

🎭 Activity: Role-Play a Pitch
Pair up and act out your first gig negotiation:
"Hi! I offer $30 logos with two free revisions. Would that fit your brand?"
Bridge to Next: You've got deals rolling — now, let's avoid burnout.

Time & Task Management

🌐 Top Tools

- Trello: Drag-and-drop boards for projects.
- Notion: Track deadlines, notes, and earnings.
- Focus Booster: 25-minute Pomodoro bursts.

⌛ Weekly Balance Plan

Area	% of Time	Example
School	70%	Classes, study sessions
Family/Friends	20%	Hangouts, rest
Gigs	10% (start)	Weekend projects

🔄 Flowchart: Gig Work Loop

START: Client Message
↓
PLAN: Brainstorm + Quote
↓ (Fits Schedule?)
YES → DO: Timer On — Execute
↓
DELIVER: Submit + Invoice
↓
REVIEW: Log Wins & Lessons
↓
REST: Recharge!
↓
→ LOOP BACK

Growth & Sustainability

Your gigs are just the beginning — this is your launchpad to portfolio power (see Chapter 9).

🚀 Turning One-Off Gigs into Repeat Clients

- After project wrap-up, pitch add-ons:
- "Loved your logo? Want social media posts too?"
- Offer discounts for referrals.

💲 Scaling Income

- Bundle services (Logo + Ad design).
- Add passive income (Etsy templates, digital planners).
- Teens who scale smart earn +50% more in 6 months.

📋 Tracking & Mini Portfolio

Keep a simple Google Doc:
- Client name
- Feedback quote
- Screenshot proof
- Earning amount

❄ Mind Map: Gig Scaling Blueprint

Center: My First Gig
- Branch 1: Clients → Repeat Work → Referrals
- Branch 2: Skills → Upsell → Passive Income
- Branch 3: Track → Feedback → Improve
- Branch 4: Balance → Review → Dream Biz

Color code: 💚 = Money Wins | 💙 = Skills | 💜 = Cautions

🎯 30-Day Challenge: Earn Your First $100

Day	Task	Reward
1–5	Set up profile	Playlist jam
6–15	Apply to gigs	Share with a friend
16–25	Deliver 2+ tasks	Treat (snack/stream)
26–30	Reflect + Plan Next	Celebrate!

- Write down your first gig idea.
- Snap your profile pic.
- DM a friend to be your practice client.

✦ You're not waiting for permission — you are the permission.
#GigTeenTakeover 🚀

CHAPTER 9: GLOBAL MINDSET — THINK BEYOND BORDERS

Chapter 9: GLOBAL MINDSET – THINK BEYOND BORDERS

Imagine filming a TikTok collab with a creator in Tokyo or brainstorming an app with a coder in São Paulo—all from your bedroom in California or New York. That's the global mindset: leveling up your digital game (from Chapters 5 and 8) by connecting across cultures, not just borders.

We're talking remote teams that span continents, gigs with clients in Berlin, and youth challenges that could land you on a UN stage. For U.S. teens—where over 70 percent already follow international creators—this chapter is your passport to global collaboration.

We'll explore the hype, decode cultural cues, and show real-world hacks to work smoothly with anyone, anywhere. By the end, you'll think, create, and lead globally—without leaving home.

Quick Stat to Fuel Your World View

In 2025, 48 percent of U.S. freelancers on Upwork worked with international clients—up 10 percent from 2024. Your next logo gig could fund a Euro trip.

What Is a Global Mindset?

A global mindset isn't a buzzword—it's your next-gen career power.

Definition

It's the ability to step outside your base culture and realize there's no single "right" way to work. It means appreciating different styles, traditions, and time zones—and using that awareness to collaborate smarter.

Why It Matters

- Global companies now build teams in 5 or more countries.
- Cross-border teamwork improves communication, empathy, and adaptability.
- Teens with global experience are twice as likely to land international internships.

Real Teen Example

Aisha, 17, from Chicago, co-founded a climate app with developers in Kenya via Discord. Her secret? "I asked about their holidays first—instant squad."

→ Bridge to Next:

Know the mindset? Now decode the signals—because a thumbs-up emoji isn't universal.

Understanding Cultural Differences

Cultural differences can make or break collaboration. Learn to read the room—even online.

Communication Cues
- Tone: U.S. = direct; Japan = polite.
- Time: Germany = punctual; Brazil = flexible.
- Gestures: High-five = OK in U.S.; not so much in India.
- Context: High-context cultures (Japan, India) read between lines; low-context (U.S., Germany) state it outright.

Table: Feedback Styles by Country

Country	Style	Tip for U.S. Teens
Japan	Indirect, harmony-focused	Add softeners like "if that works for you?"
Brazil	Expressive, relationship-first	Start with small talk—build rapport first
Germany	Direct, data-driven	Be concise and fact-based
India	Respectful, context-rich	Use polite phrasing and titles

- → **Bridge to Next:**

Cues cracked? Time to sync your clocks and languages—because 3 a.m. DMs rarely impress.

Working Across Time Zones and Languages

Planning Hacks
- Use World Time Buddy to find "golden hours."
- Prefer asynchronous (async) tools—such as Loom videos or Slack threads.
- Leverage your U.S. time zone, as it overlaps with both Europe and Asia.

Free Tool Kit
- DeepL – accurate, slang-friendly translations
- Grammarly – tone and clarity checks
- Notion – shared workspace
- Clockify – track global work hours
- Duolingo – learn basics of another language (10 min a day!)

Real Example
Mia, 15, from Texas, worked with a French coder on Fiverr.
Using DeepL for project notes cut two weeks of confusion and earned her a 5-star review.

Simple Flowchart

START → Message Sent
↓
TRANSLATE → Check for Clarity
↓
COLLABORATE → Share on Notion + Confirm Time
↓
DELIVER → Use Loom for Demo
↓
FEEDBACK → Adjust & Repeat

→ **Bridge to Next:**
Now that you can communicate worldwide, let's learn to represent yourself responsibly online.

Digital Citizenship and Etiquette

Online respect travels farther than Wi-Fi.

Core Rules

1. Respect – Ask: "Would I say this in person?"
2. Empathy – Consider how humor or tone lands across cultures.
3. Safety – Enable 2-factor auth, verify sources, report scams.

Avoid Stereotypes & Misinfo

A U.S. teen once assumed "siesta = lazy." After asking, she learned it's a productivity reset. Curiosity beats judgment.

Build Your Global Brand

- LinkedIn headline: "U.S. teen coder | AI for Good enthusiast."
- Discord/Slack Bio: "NYC student | K-drama fan | Open to cross-continent projects."

- Include a thank-you or cultural nod ("Appreciate Berlin feedback!").

→ Bridge to Next:
- Etiquette locked in? Let's explore global opportunities waiting for you.

Joining Global Opportunities

Where to Find Them
- UN Youth Dialogue – virtual panels on AI & equality (free)
- AI for Good Youth Zone – tech workshops for SDGs
- Global Youth AI Innovation Challenge – themes: climate & ethics
- Teens in AI Techathon – demo days for girls in STEM

Application Tip
Write a 200-word statement:
"As a Seattle gamer, I want to design inclusive VR worlds for kids in India — bridging fun and learning."

Real Teen Success
Sofia, 16, from Miami, co-created a disaster-response robot with a Kenyan team.

Her prototype reached the finals of the 2025 AI for Good Summit.

Activity — Create Your "Global You" Map

Center: You (Name + Hometown)
- Languages → English, Español (basic)
- Interests → Gaming → Global Twist: Eco apps for Asia
- Future Countries → Japan (tech) | Brazil (design)
- Connections → Discord pals in Germany → Next step: Reach out

Color code: Blue = skills, Green = dreams.

Reflection and Application

Journal Prompt
"What did I learn from another culture today?"
Example: "Japanese 'wa' = harmony → less drama in group chats."

Peer Exchange Challenge
Find a non-U.S. teen via PenPal World or Discord #GlobalYouth.
Swap a day-in-the-life video, then brainstorm a mini-project like "sustainable snacks."

Trivia Corner
The world's youngest delegate at the 2025 UNFCCC talks was Prasiddhi Singh, 14, from India—proof that teens already shape policy.

⊕ Chapter Wrap-Up
You've blurred borders and built bridges.
This chapter connects directly to your Chapter 8 gigs and Chapter 10 launch plans, unlocking an international edge.

Key Takeaway Checklist
- ✅ Defined your global mindset
- ✅ Learned one cultural tip per country
- ✅ Practiced the flowchart for online collabs
- ✅ Mapped your "Global You" plan
- ✅ Reflected or connected with a peer abroad

Call to Action
Choose one tool today—DeepL a message, join AI for Good, or DM a global friend:
"What's one hack from your world?"
Share your map with #GlobalTeenBlueprint.

The planet is your playground—own it. 🌐✨

CHAPTER 10: PASSION PROJECTS — TURN IDEAS INTO IMPACT

Chapter 10: PASSION PROJECTS – TURN IDEAS INTO IMPACT

Theme: Transform What You Love Into Real-World Change

Ever doodled a wild app idea during math class or ranted about ocean plastic to your squad?

That's your spark — now fan it into a full-on fire.

Passion projects aren't homework; they're your secret weapon to mix hobbies with world-changer energy. They prove you're not just smart — you're driven.
Linking back to your self-scan (Chapter 1), digital skills (Chapter 5), gigs (Chapter 8), and global mindset (Chapter 9), this chapter is your DIY lab:

Spot the idea → Blueprint it → Launch it → Turn it into portfolio gold.

Quick Stat to Spark Your Fire:

A 2025 College Board report shows 65% of admissions officers say personal projects demonstrate commitment and authenticity better than club memberships — making them a top differentiator for college apps.
Your move? Own it.

What Is a Passion Project?

A passion project is your brainchild — no grades attached, all heart-fueled.
It's your side quest, the one you chase because it matters to you.

Definition & Examples: A passion project is a self-initiated creation that blends your interests, skills, and purpose.
It could be:
- A school eco-club is organizing beach cleanups in Miami.
- A YouTube series reviewing indie games from your Seattle basement.
- An app prototype that tracks allergies for your diabetic sibling in Texas.

Real Teen Wins

- Nidhi Bhaskar, from California, launched New Boundaries for Youth, a nonprofit that runs sustainability contests for Indian middle-schoolers — and was accepted to Brown University's 7-year med program (PLME, acceptance rate <2%).
- A Texas teen designed a water-purifying backpack — scored praise from President Obama and later won Harvard science recognition.

Why They Matter

Passion projects show initiative, leadership, and authenticity — traits colleges, employers, and global organizations value most.

◆ Fact: 65% of top college admits highlight a personal project in essays — it's their "Tell me who you are" moment.

→ **Bridge to Next:**

Ready to find your cause? Let's turn late-night ideas into action.

Finding Your Cause or Idea

Can't pick one thing? Start simple:
Ask yourself — What bugs me? What excites me? What would I fix if I could?
Identifying What Excites You
List out:

- Issues (climate change, mental health, inclusivity)
- Hobbies (music, design, gaming, writing)
- Skills (video editing, coding, photography, storytelling)

◎ Tip: According to 2025 YPulse data, 1 in 5 U.S. high schoolers is already active in youth-led causes.

Connecting Passion with Purpose

Combine your interests for a bigger impact:
- 🎨 Art + Environment → Mural series from recycled materials
- 🎮 Gaming + Mental Health → Roblox world for anxiety coping
- 🤖 AI + Ethics → Podcast series on fairness in algorithms

Real Example:

16-year-old Mia Patel built "Mindful Maps," a Roblox space to help teens decompress — pitched it at TEDxYouth.

Mind Map: From Passion to Impact

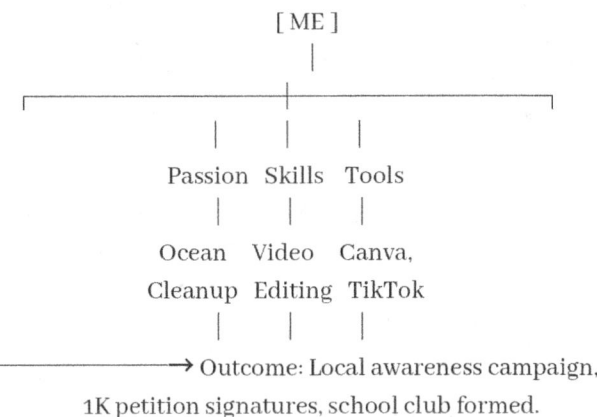

🎨 Activity: Sketch your own Passion Map using paper or Canva.

Color-code: Red = Passions | Blue = Skills | Green = Tools | Gold = Impact.

Bridge to Next
→ Got your map? Let's turn dreams into a plan.

From Idea to Action Plan

Time to move from "cool idea" to "actual impact."
Here's where your SMART goals come in — a framework from Chapter 6.

Setting SMART Goals

SMART Step	Example
Specific	Launch 3 eco-murals in school courtyard
Measurable	Seen by 500 students
Achievable	Use school art supplies
Relevant	Raise awareness for recycling
Time-bound	Complete by Spring Break

📊 Teens who set SMART goals hit 42% more milestones, according to 2025 productivity research.

Mini Project Planner

Step	Tool	Time Frame	Output Example
Idea	Journal / Notion	Week 1	"Plastic Waste Mural" sketch
Research	Google Scholar / YouTube	Weeks 2–3	10 stats + 3 inspiration videos
Build	Canva / Paint	Weeks 4–6	3 mural prototypes + photo log
Share	Instagram / School Site	Week 7	Post event invite + thread

Flowchart: From Spark to Showcase

START → SPARK → RESEARCH → BUILD → SHARE → REFLECT → REVISE/EXPAND

💡 Pro Tip: Treat this like a loop — every project evolves after reflection.

Bridge to Next →
Ready to show the world? Time to share it smart.

Showcasing and Sharing

Hidden gems don't shine — your project deserves the spotlight.

Creating Visibility

Use digital tools to build your audience:
- Blog – WordPress or Medium for updates
- Video – CapCut or Canva for behind-the-scenes clips
- Slides – Google Slides for school or contest pitches

Teen Win Example:

A NY teen built "Brabble," a Braille-learning game, posted updates on LinkedIn, and earned SUNY honors recognition.

Feedback & Testimonials

Ask: "What worked? What can improve?"
Capture praise or reviews for your portfolio.
Example: "This app helped me manage anxiety — game changer!"

Activity: 30-Day Impact Challenge

Day	Task	Goal
1	Post teaser of your idea	Announce your project
15	Share progress video	Gain 50 engagements
30	Reveal final result + tag peers	Hit 100 interactions

Bridge to Next

→ You've shared your work — now let's reflect and grow.

Reflecting and Measuring Growth

Journaling Progress
Log weekly highlights:
- 🎯 Milestone: "Hit 200 views!"
- ✖ Mistake: "Edited too much, lost authenticity."
- 💬 Lesson: "Next time, keep it real."

✓ Reflective teens report 30% higher confidence, says a 2025 youth psychology study.

Presenting Your Project

Show your creation at:
- Science Fairs: Regeneron ISEF
- Innovation Contests: Prudential Emerging Visionaries
- Online Spaces: Reddit r/TeenProjects or Discord groups

Turning It Into Portfolio Gold

Add to your LinkedIn, college essays, or gig portfolios.

Frame it like this:
"Led a 6-week eco-art project viewed by 500+ peers. Resulted in school recycling policy updates."

Prompt:
"How did this project change how I see myself?"
Example: "From 'art kid' to 'impact artist' — now I chase collabs, not likes."

Closing Chapter: Your Future Blueprint

Full circle — from Chapter 1's self-scan to Chapter 9's global collabs, your passion project is proof of transformation.

Connect the Dots
Self-Assessment → Skill Practice → Gig Work → Global Collaboration → Impact Project.

Step	Done?	Notes / Next Step
Mind Map Sketched	[ ]	Add 1 new branch
SMART Goals Set	[ ]	Review progress biweekly
Timeline Followed	[ ]	Adjust if needed
Shared + Feedback	[ ]	Collect 5 testimonials
Journaled Reflection	[ ]	Update portfolio
Pitched to Opportunity	[ ]	Apply to 1 fair or contest

Motivational Note

Your journey starts now.
The blueprint's not a plan on paper — it's a living legacy in motion.
That mural? That app? That club?
It's your story's first spark — the start of something bigger.
Go messy. Go bold. Go build.
The world has room for your fire. 🔥

Chapter Wrap-Up

- ✅ Defined your project type
- ✅ Created your mind map
- ✅ Built your action flowchart
- ✅ Shared through the 30-Day Challenge
- ✅ Reflected and logged lessons

Call to Action:

Pick one checklist step today — sketch that map, DM a collab partner, or post your teaser.
Tag #TeenPassionImpact — your next chapter begins when you press share.

CHAPTER 11 : APPENDIX

Chapter 11 : APPENDIX

Table A1: Fast-Growth Career Paths for Teens (No Degree Needed to Start)

Career Path	What You Actually Do	Beginner Starting Point	Realistic Teen Starter Earnings
Social Media Content Editor	Edit TikTok/Reels for small brands	Learn CapCut + Canva	$10–$50/video
AI Prompt Creator	Write prompts to generate images/text	Practice on ChatGPT / PromptHero	$5–$30/prompt pack
Freelance Tutor (Online)	Help younger students in your best subject	Use Zoom + Free whiteboard tools	$8–$20/hr
Reseller / Thrift Flipper	Buy items cheap + resell online	Platforms: Depop / Poshmark	$50–$300/month starter
Website Builder (No-Code)	Create simple websites for local shops	Learn Carrd or Wix	$30–$200/site

Table A2: Best Free Platforms to Learn In-Demand Digital Skills

Skill Area	Free Platform	Best Starter Course	Time to Beginner Skill
Graphic Design	Canva Design School	"Getting Started with Canva"	2–5 hours
Coding (Web)	freeCodeCamp	"Responsive Web Design"	10–20 hours
Data & Analytics	Google Analytics Academy	"Google Analytics for Beginners"	6–12 hours
AI & Prompting	DeepLearning.AI (Coursera audit free)	"ChatGPT Prompting Essentials"	4–8 hours
Video Editing	DaVinci Resolve (YouTube official tutorials)	"Resolve Beginner Series"	6–12 hours

Table A3: Beginner-Friendly Gig Platforms for Teens (Age Requirements Included)

Platform	What You Can Sell	Age Requirement	Safety Note
Fiverr	Art, edits, writing, thumbnails	13+ (with parent consent)	Use app messaging — no off-platform DM
Etsy	Printables, handmade crafts, stickers	13+ (with parent shop owner)	Use parental bank account setup
Discord / Instagram DMs	Community support, editing help	No age lock	Never send personal info
Wyzant / Preply	Tutoring	18+	Teens can still tutor privately or via school
Upwork	Professional freelance	18+	Teens start on Fiverr first, then upgrade

Table A4: Quick Matching – Personality to Gig Type

Personality Type	Strengths	Best Gig Matches	Why It Fits
Creative / Expressive	Visual storytelling	Thumbnail design, Reels editing	Fast projects + portfolio growth
Analytical / Problem-Solver	Patterns & logic	Coding mini apps, data tasks	Clear tasks and measurable progress
Social / Outgoing	Communication & confidence	Tutoring, hosting study groups	People-first work = instant results
Independent / Quiet	Focused solo work	Etsy digital products, blogging	Work alone, scale with time

Table A5: Free Tools Every Teen Creator Should Know

Purpose	Tool Name	Why It's Useful	Difficulty
Graphic Design	Canva	Drag-and-drop templates	Easy
Video Editing	CapCut	Mobile-friendly editing	Easy
Idea Planning	Notion	All-in-one workspace	Medium
Website Portfolio	Carrd	Free & aesthetic 1-page sites	Easy
File Sharing	Google Drive	Share work professionally	Easy

Table A6: Global Communication Cheat Sheet

Region / Culture	Typical Communication Style	How to Adapt When Working With Them
U.S. & Canada	Direct & quick	Say what you need clearly and fast
Japan & South Korea	Polite + indirect	Use softer wording ("Maybe we could try…")
Germany & Netherlands	Very direct + factual	Give reasons + data, not vague opinions
Brazil & Philippines	Friendly + relationship-first	Start with small talk before tasks

Table A7: 10 Passion Project Ideas Teens Can Start in One Week

Project Idea	Tools Needed	Final Output	Portfolio Value
"Study Skills Tip" TikTok series	Phone + CapCut	10 short videos	Shows communication & consistency
Local "Clean-Up Challenge" Event	Canva flyer	Photos + recap post	Shows leadership & community impact
Mini Podcast (3 episodes)	Anchor.fm	Audio link	Shows voice, ideas & discipline
Classroom Notes Blog	Google Sites	Study resource hub	Shows initiative + academic strength
Fan Art / Moodboard Page	Pinterest + Canva	Art gallery page	Shows creativity + personal style
Simple Website for a Local Shop	Carrd / Wix	Live website	Shows real-world service
Mini eBook ("How to Survive 9th Grade")	Google Docs → PDF	5–10 page guide	Shows writing + mentoring ability
School Club Logo Redesign	Canva	Before/after showcase	Shows design improvement ability
Healthy Snack Recipe Book	Phone photos + Google Docs	PDF booklet	Shows wellness + content creation
VR "Chill Room" in Roblox	Roblox Studio	Shareable world link	Shows 3D + teamwork

Table A8: College & Scholarship Essay Power Verbs (Use in Applications & Resumes)

Verb	When to Use It	Example
Led	When you organized something	"Led a community clean-up program"
Designed	When you created something	"Designed brand assets for a student club"
Launched	When you started a project	"Launched a tutoring channel for Algebra I"
Improved	When you made something better	"Improved study notes system for classmates"
Collaborated	When you worked with others	"Collaborated with peers across 3 time zones"

Table A9: Best Websites for Teen Internships & Remote Opportunities

Website	Focus Area	Why It's Good
Forage.com	Virtual job experience programs	Lets you try careers before choosing them
DoSomething.org	Social & volunteer causes	Great for activism & leadership experience
TeensInAI.com	AI hackathons & workshops	Global collabs for tech-minded students
Smithsonian Open Access	Creative & history projects	Use real museum data for research projects

Table A10: Monthly Progress Reflection Prompt Set

Reflection Focus	Guiding Question	What to Note
Growth	What skill improved this month?	Be specific ("I can now edit audio cleanly")
Challenges	What was hardest?	Describe, don't judge
Next Step	What small improvement will I make next month?	Keep it tiny and clear

CONCLUSION: YOUR BLUEPRINT IS THE BEGINNING

You've just built something most people don't create until their late twenties:
clarity, direction, and a plan.
This wasn't just a workbook.

It was a mirror, a map, and a launchpad.
- In Chapter 1, you learned who you are—your strengths, values, and energy style.
- In Chapters 2–4, you learned how to talk about your goals and explore real career paths—not the old "doctor/lawyer/engineer only" script, but future-focused roles in digital media, sustainability, AI, design, and innovation.
- In Chapter 5, you unlocked digital leverage—free tools that turn ideas into action.
- In Chapter 6, you built your Personal Education Plan—your roadmap instead of "just winging it."
- In Chapter 7, you saw real teens already winning—and why age is no barrier.
- In Chapter 8, you learned how to earn your first dollars through gigs that fit your personality.
- In Chapter 9, you expanded your world—collaborating across cultures and borders.
- In Chapter 10, you learned how to turn your passion into your impact.

This is more than preparation. To begin. To experiment. To change directions when needed. To grow publicly.

The World You're Entering Is Different

Jobs now shift faster than trends. Careers evolve. Skills update constantly.

But you are ready because you now know how to:
- Learn quickly
- Adapt and experiment
- Build real skills
- Earn independently
- Collaborate globally
- Create opportunities instead of waiting for them

This is the real career advantage.

Your Next Step (Simple, Clear, Today)
1. Choose one gig, skill, or project from this book.
2. Start it within 48 hours.
3. Track your progress for 30 days.

Small steps beat perfect plans.

Remember This
- You don't need to be the best to begin.
- You don't need permission to create.
- You don't need to wait for adulthood to start shaping your future.

Your blueprint is not fixed. Update it. Upgrade it. Rewrite it as you evolve. Your Future Isn't Something You Find. It's something you build.

- One skill.
- One connection.
- One bold step at a time.

The world is not waiting to choose you.
It is waiting for you to choose yourself.

Go build. Go learn. Go launch.
Your story starts now.

Dr. Fanatomy

CHECK MY OTHER BOOKS .....